SHO

MOORS

PAUL HANNON

HILLSIDE PUBLICATIONS
2 New School Lane, Cullingworth, Bradford BD13 5DA

First Published 2022   © Paul Hannon 2022

ISBN 978 1 907626 43 2

Sketch maps based on OS 1947 1-inch maps

Cover illustrations: Greenberfield; Pendle Hill from Roughlee
Back cover: Haslingden Grane; Page 1: Foulridge Wharf
(Paul Hannon/Yorkshire Photo Library)

Printed in China on behalf of Latitude Press

HILLSIDE GUIDES... cover much of Northern England

- 50 Yorkshire Walks For All   • Journey of the Wharfe (photobook)

Short Scenic Walks • Teesdale & Weardale • Ribble Valley & Bowland
- Wharfedale & Ilkley • Three Peaks & Malham • Arnside & Lunesdale
- North York Moors   • Harrogate & Nidderdale   • South Pennines
- Wensleydale & Swaledale   • Ambleside & South Lakeland
- Pendle & Lancashire Moors   • Aire Valley   • Haworth

Walking in Yorkshire
- North York Moors South & West
- Nidderdale & Ripon
- Wharfedale & Malham
- Aire Valley & Bronte Country
- Yorkshire Wolds
- South Yorkshire

- Three Peaks & Howgill Fells
- North York Moors North & East
- Wensleydale & Swaledale
- Harrogate & Ilkley
- Howardian Hills & Vale of York
- Calderdale & South Pennines
- West Yorkshire Countryside

Lancashire/Cumbria • Pendle & the Ribble   • Eden Valley

Long Distance • Dales Way • Coast to Coast Walk • Pendle Way

Visit us at www.hillsidepublications.co.uk

CONTENTS

Thursden Brook

Gill church, Barnoldswick

INTRODUCTION

The old milltowns of Lancashire sit among splendid walking country, with an array of colourful landscapes rolling from the celebrated Pendle Hill around to the West Pennine Moors.

The Pendle district offers cosy villages such as Newchurch and Kelbrook nestled among sheep pastures, with the ever-popular Leeds-Liverpool Canal meandering through. The Pennine backbone to the east is dominated by Boulsworth Hill, while the surrounds of Hurstwood and Thursden lead around to Thieveley Pike and the heights dividing Burnley and Blackburn to the north from Rochdale, Bury and Bolton to the south. Amid all this the absorbing Rossendale Valley with the heights of Great Hameldon and Cribden merges into the West Pennine Moors, whose best known features include Winter Hill and Haslingden Grane.

These walks fully embrace this wide geographical spread, with routes to countless places of interest. Abandoned industrial hamlets like White Coppice and Wycoller form characterful backwaters, while there is evidence of small-scale quarrying and collieries on the moors. Splendid woodland is found at Sunnyhurst and Lever Park, with relaxing reservoir walking at Watergrove, Anglezarke and Jumbles. Fascinating side valleys feature at Healey Dell, Shedden Clough and Musbury Clough, with fine historic buildings at Turton Tower, Rivington and Helmshore Textile Museum. Modern art of The Halo and the Singing Ringing Tree has joined the more traditional stone towers of Darwen Moor, Holcombe Moor and Rivington. While the sight and sound of industry and urbanisation may never be far away, it will usually seem like it is once you set foot on the Lancashire Moors.

Almost all walks are on rights of way or established access areas and paths: a handful which cross Open Access land are noted as such. Whilst the route description should be sufficient to guide you around, a map offers greater information and interest: Ordnance Survey Explorer maps OL21 and 287 cover the walks.

Information
- Pendle Heritage Centre **Barrowford** BB9 6JQ (01282-677150)
- 28 Deardengate **Haslingden** Rossendale BB4 5QJ (07590-434002)
- West Pennine Moors, Great House Information Centre **Rivington** Bolton BL6 7SB (01204-691549)

PENDLE & the LANCASHIRE MOORS

30 Short Scenic Walks

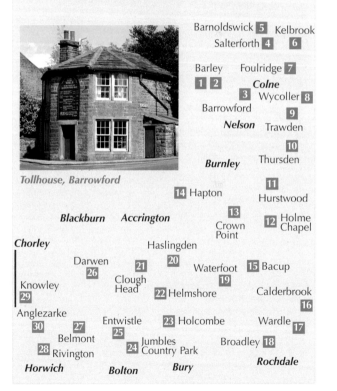

Tollhouse, Barrowford

Barnoldswick **5** Kelbrook

Salterforth **4** **6**

Barley Foulridge **7**

1 **2** *Colne*

3 Wycoller **8**

Barrowford **9**

Nelson Trawden

10

Burnley Thursden

11

Hurstwood

14 Hapton

13 **12** Holme
Chapel

Blackburn *Accrington*

Crown
Point

Chorley Haslingden

Darwen **20**

26 **21** Waterfoot **15** Bacup

Clough **19**

Knowley Head Calderbrook

29 **22** Helmshore

16

Anglezarke Entwistle **23** Holcombe Wardle **17**

30 **27** **25**

Belmont **24** Jumbles Broadley **18**

28 Rivington Country Park

Horwich *Bolton* *Bury* *Rochdale*

4¾ miles from Barley

A classic ascent from the village in its lap: a must!

Start Village centre (SD 823403; BB12 9JX), car park
Map OS Explorer OL21, South Pennines (**or** Explorer OL41)

Cradled under Pendle Hill, Barley has the Pendle Inn, Barley Mow, tearooms, WC and information centre. From the car park entrance turn right over the bridge, then cross to a side road past the village hall at Barley Green. Alongside is imposing Barley Green Farmhouse as the road runs on into Ogden Clough. Rising to the dam of Lower Ogden Reservoir, either remain on the road, or take a small gate just a little further sending a concession path by the shore. It continues beyond the reservoir head, initially broader and near the stream, to reach a gate back onto the rougher road just short of the upper dam. Through a gate a stony pull up the right side of the dam leads to Upper Ogden Reservoir.

A path resumes along its northern shore, crossing a wall at a kissing-gate to amble amid bracken for a grand walk along the clough floor. Kissing-gates in a fence then a wall put you onto the moor proper. The path briefly climbs right before contouring on to Boar Clough. Ford the stream and bear right up the initially rough path above the clough edge: it soon improves and eases on the rim of the clough. Now amid open moorland, the path rises gradually to approach the now insignificant clough. Fording the streamlet above a rocky bed, the path soon bears away right. Superfluous cairns confirm the clear, gently-graded route as the path becomes grassy underfoot, with views opening out left to Longridge, Parlick and Fair Snape Fells. Further, it curves up to the left to merge into a wide, stony path, though a thin parallel option runs just yards further, overlooking the eastern escarpment. A final, short pull reveals the OS column at 1827ft/557m. A perch on the rim of the mighty drop enjoys a bird's-eye view over Barley in its fold of the hills. Pendle Hill's isolation earns an extensive panorama, with the South and West Pennine moors beyond the East Lancashire towns, and a long Dales skyline to the north including all Three Peaks.

Leave by heading north the short way to a wall with a stone shelter, either on the stony path or again above the edge. On meeting the wall the main path goes right with it just as far as a stile, then doubles back to commence its descent: the edge path quickly merges. This strengthened path undertakes a sustained slant to a wall corner, then down with the wall to a gate off the fell. Slant right behind Pendle House to a corner gate, from where a firm path descends a fieldside to a kissing-gate. Bear right down the next field to a bridle-gate, and a firm path runs to another in a wall. A concession path drops away with a fence the short way to a track between houses at Brown House. From a kissing-gate ahead, drop past the right-hand house onto an enclosed streamside path. The stream is twice crossed as the path runs unfailingly down onto a lane. Go left past a house and café at Ings End, and just a little further, at a bend, take a footbridge on the right. Turn down the final field as Barley's roofs appear ahead, and at the far corner a footbridge is crossed before becoming enclosed for the final steps onto the village street.

Looking east from Pendle Hill

4 miles from Barley

Stunning Pendle views in the very heart of Witch Country

BARLEY · Narrowgates · White Hough
Ogden Clough · S
Fell Wood
Driver Height
NEWCHURCH

Start Village centre
(SD 823403; BB12 9JX), car park
Map *OS Explorer OL21, South Pennines (**or** Explorer OL41)*

For a note on Barley see page 6. From the car park entrance turn right over the bridge, then cross to a side road past the village hall at Barley Green. Alongside is Barley Green Farmhouse as the road runs on past a former 1912 filter house into Ogden Clough. Rising to the dam of Lower Ogden Reservoir, either remain on the road, or take a small gate just a little further sending a concession path by the shore. It continues beyond the reservoir head, initially broader and near the stream, to reach a gate back onto the rougher road just short of the upper dam. Through a gate a stony pull up the right side of the dam leads to Upper Ogden Reservoir. Cross the dam to a bridle-gate onto the foot of rough moorland, and a path ascends moist, reedy terrain to join a crumbling wall to the left. Look back to a fine profile of Pendle's eastern scarp, and into the recesses of Ogden Clough.

Around the point you merge with the wall beneath Driver Height, a fence-stile sends a level path away to a corner wall-stile off the grassy moor. A thin path crosses to meet a wall enclosing Fell Wood, and this leads over a gentle brow from where suburban East Lancashire appears beneath a moorland skyline. From a corner stile at the wood end, go straight ahead with a fence on your left, through a crumbled wall and on with a wall to a gentle brow. To your left is Lower Ogden Reservoir again, with Barley backed by the Black Moss reservoirs. Continue to another stile, and briefly with the descending wall to a stile just beyond a gate. Here bear right across this larger pasture, dropping to a small gate near the bottom corner into woodland. A clear path drops the short way down the wood edge to a kissing-gate into Newchurch. St Mary's church tower dates from 1544: near the porch is the 'witch's grave', reputedly that of Alice Nutter. Also in this tiny hillside village is a unique shop, 'Witches Galore', and WC. Keep left up Cross Lane, past the houses to a bend at the top. Mighty Pendle Hill returns in all its glory, overlooking Barley.

Turn right here along the Barley Fold drive, but leave almost at once by a gate in front, following the wall along the broad ridge outside a wood. Part way along, a stile admits into the trees and a path slants down to a stile at the end. Emerging reveals big views over the environs of Roughlee and Blacko. Head away to rejoin the ridge-wall on the left, and follow this down Thorny Bank outside another plantation. A corner-stile at the wood end sends a little path down the wall's other side to a gate onto an enclosed track. From one opposite, descend a field to a gate onto a road, crossing to descend an access road over a bridge on Pendle Water to the hamlet of White Hough. As it swings upstream, keep left of the houses to narrow into a firm track through grand surrounds to Narrowgates. Two rows of weavers' cottages precede a cotton mill closed in the 1960s: note the preserved chimney. Just beyond, a path goes forward to Barley's car park.

Newchurch church

3½ miles from Barrowford

A nice old village sits between big views and a streamside stroll

Start Heritage centre *(SD 862397; BB9 6JQ), car park across road*

Map *OS Explorer OL21, South Pennines (**or** Explorer OL41)*

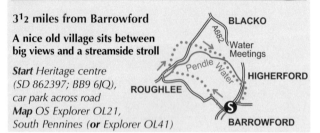

Pendle Heritage Centre is based in 17th century Park Hill, and has shop, tearoom, exhibitions, 14th century cruck barn and walled gardens. Over the bridge in this bustling village is a toll-house of 1805, complete with notice of tolls. From the centre a path runs through the park behind it, alongside Pendle Water to a footbridge. Cross it and the parallel A682, and up the side of the 17th century White Bear. Continue up past most of the housing to a sharp bend, then go straight ahead on Pasture House farm drive. Over to the right is Stansfield Tower on Blacko Hill. Halfway up, beyond allotments, take a small gate on the left and head off with a fence. Quickly go right over a footbridge to rise by an old hedge-line. Higher, it becomes loosely enclosed by trees to reach a barn, with the abandoned farmhouse of West Pasture just to the right.

From a stile/gate ahead, ascend a field with a fading line of trees, and a little higher you gain a brow to reveal a grand prospect dominated by Pendle Hill: Roughlee appears below on reaching a wall-stile at the end. Slant gently left down the field past a lone tree, a little path forming to descend more directly to a bank at the bottom, dropping left to stepping-stones on Pendle Water. Behind, the road is joined at a stile, where go briefly left into Roughlee. Just short of the Bay Horse pub by the bridge, double back right along the front of a row of white cottages immediately off a junction with Stang Top Road. This narrows to run by the front of Roughlee Old Hall, a fine house with mullioned windows: it was reputedly home to Alice Nutter, a 'lady' among the clutch of Pendle Witches.

Turn up the drive at the end, through Hollin Farm and on to a house at Middlewood just beyond. Through a kissing-gate ahead, advance along a hedgerowed way to a small gate at the end. Just beyond is a small corner gate, from which resume with a fence to a small gate onto a road behind a barn. From one almost opposite, head away on a wooded bank above Pendle Water. Just short of the top, take a path right to run through open terrain at mid-height above the stream. Arriving almost at its bank, you part company again to head on through marshy terrain preceding a distinct bend. Escaping reeds, maintain height to cross to a small gate in a hedge ahead. The way keeps to this height above a wooded bank, opening out to descend open pasture towards Water Meetings. Bear left to a footbridge on Blacko Water, and turn downstream on a forming track to the lovely confluence with Pendle Water.

The track runs on to a gate onto an access road at a bridge. Across, turn downstream for a grand walk on a firm, enclosed path to Higherford, passing isolated Old Oak Tree Cottage. At the end it joins residential Barleydale Road: keep on to historic Higherford Bridge just round the corner. Cross this to cobbled Pinfold and onto the main road. Cross and turn right past the Old Bridge pub, immediately after which take a path tracing the wooded stream back to the car park.

Pendle Water above Water Meetings

4³4 miles from Salterforth

Very easy walking focussed on a colourful waterway

Start Anchor Inn
(SD 887453; BB18 5TT), Salterforth Moorings car park across road
Map OS Explorer OL21,
South Pennines

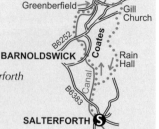

Join the canal across the road from the Anchor, and head away past Salterforth Moorings for 2¹4 miles of towpath walking. The Leeds-Liverpool Canal runs 127¹4 miles between its two great city termini. Fully opened in 1816, its engineers took advantage of the Aire Gap to breach the Pennines by way of a chain of locks, only resorting to tunnelling at nearby Foulridge. The canal swings under the B6383 Barnoldswick-Kelbrook road at Park Bridge, and is followed to the arched Cockshott Bridge, alongside which is Lower Park Marina. En route you pass a forlorn stone abutment of the Barnoldswick branch line, which ran for less than two miles from the Skipton-Colne railway and closed in 1965.

At the next bridge, cross both road and canal to resume on the other bank. Leading on with gardens opposite, beneath Coates Bridge it runs between a Rolls-Royce factory and the modern housing of Coates. Entering open countryside, modern housing still occupies the opposite bank. Swinging round beneath the arched Greenberfield Bridge, you arrive at Greenberfield Locks. This set of three locks lift the canal to its highest altitude, which extends for several miles back through Salterforth to beyond Foulridge Tunnel. This is a lovely setting, with refreshments in the adjacent car park.

Advance just beyond the first lock, then take a stile onto the adjacent road. Turn right to cross the canal bridge with the central lock to your left, and up towards the B6252. Just yards before it bear left on the parallel old road through trees, dropping to meet the road approaching another Rolls-Royce factory. Advance briefly on the footway, then at the entrance gate cross to a kissing-gate opposite. A little path rises past Gill Hall: dating from the 16th century, it has an array of mullioned and transomed windows. Continue on the fieldside above the wooded cleft of The Gill to a stile at the end into the churchyard of St Mary-le-Gill (or Ghyll). Pass round to the right to the church front, with its large 16th century tower and sprawling roof. The interior features a splendid arrangement of box-pews and an awesome three-decker pulpit.

From the gateway go right on the access road, but quickly turn left on Ghyll Lane serving several houses to end at Bentham Lodge. From a small gate ahead, take a thin fieldside path left, veering right at the end to a small gate. A fenceside track runs to a gate onto a farm track: cross this and the next field, bearing left to a bridle-gate near the far left corner. With Rain Hall Farm to your right, cross another track and bear gently right across the field to a far corner gate. Don't use it, but from the adjacent stile head right with a fence to a stile onto Salterforth Lane, a rough road. Go a few strides left to a kissing-gate on the right, and head away on a good wallside path. This drops down to run to successive bridle-gates at Cockshott Bridge. Turn left to retrace the towpath to the Anchor.

At Greenberfield Locks

4¾ miles from Barnoldswick

A bracing ascent of a local landmark with a moorland return

Start Bancroft Mill (SD 875461; BB18 5QR), south-west of town centre, roadside parking
Map *OS Explorer OL21, South Pennines (**or** Explorer OL41)*

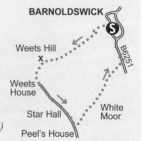

Locally 'Barlick', this independent little town is based around attractive Town Square. Bancroft Mill with its brick chimney is home to a rare steam engine that draws visitors when in operation. From the mill turn briefly left (towards town), then go left on Moorgate Road. This quickly leaves suburbia to continue as Folly Lane, soon zigzagging steeply uphill. Just past Lower Standridge Farm, take a stile by a gate on the right and resume up the lush fieldside. This grand uphill stride passes through a gate/stile, and a clearer path forms before another stile as the going eases. The terrain changes to grassy moorland above a colourful steep bank. The steeper work is accomplished to leave a very gentle stride, and through a final stile the scant remains of a circular pillar stand atop a small ravine. All this stage enjoys panoramic views north to the Yorkshire Dales and across the Ribble Valley to Bowland: in late summer the scent of heather wafts from the adjacent moorland.

Just short of the flat top, the main path swings right to a sprawling cairn, with the Ordnance Survey column just beyond. At 1302ft/397m Weets Hill not surprisingly offers a stunning view, further enhanced by the trig. point's location on the northern edge of the plateau. Barnoldswick is still in view, though the prospect north to the shapely pairing of Ingleborough and Penyghent is the highlight. To the west Pendle Hill is dramatically revealed, with Longridge Fell behind and then the Bowland massif. Another path returns to the wallside to descend the short way onto Gisburn Old Road at a gate off the hill. A short-lived green way runs to isolated Weets House: the road was a major packhorse route prior to the construction of the turnpike below - the present A682. Follow this quiet cul-de-sac road for almost a mile past several houses, with some good verges. This leisurely stroll gives ample time to survey a wide sweep of East Lancashire, with Boulsworth Hill leading round to the moors above Burnley, and Pendle Hill further right.

Shortly before isolated Peel's House, take a kissing-gate on the left just beyond an earlier signed path. Head away on a rough wallside track to quickly reach the beginning of the walled green lane of Lister Well Road. Down below are the Foulridge reservoirs, while Great Edge, Kelbrook Moor and Elslack Moor sit across the valley. Lister Well Road provides a gem of a stroll alongside the rampant heather carpet of White Moor. This way rolls on for some time, gradually declining until commencing a more pronounced descent. After absorbing Prospect Farm drive, continue down to ultimately emerge onto the B6251 Barnoldswick-Foulridge road. Go left and left again on Gillians Lane, which leads quickly back to the start.

The summit of Weets Hill, looking to Pendle Hill

4¹⁄₂ miles from Kelbrook

Rolling hills and heather moors

Start *Village centre (SD 902447; BB18 6TF), roadside parking*
Map *OS Explorer OL21, South Pennines*

Leave on Vicarage Road opposite the Craven Heifer, onto Main Street with St Mary's church to your left. Follow Dotcliffe Road ahead with Harden Beck on your left: as it swings right branch left over the beck, leaving the village as Heads Lane rising between hedgerows. Ending at Heads House Farm, a cart track passes through a gate ahead to rise pleasantly away. Ending at a gateway into a field after bridging a streamlet, ascend the fieldside to a gate. Continue on the grassy way up a field centre, and on through two gates. Keep right of a ditch, past a wall corner to a corner gate just beyond. Through this, leave the rising path and contour right to a stile in a facing wall above the tree-lined beck.

A faint trod crosses rough pasture to a gateway, with a foot-bridge on the stream just ahead. Across it the little path rises away, swinging left to a house at Harden Clough. From a stile into its garden, pass left of the house down to a gate onto its drive. Across it a footbridge sends a path slanting right up a steep, colourful bank, with Kelbrook Wood across the stream. Above a wall-stile the path rises to Scald Bank: pass left of the house on a track to join its ascending drive. As it swings left take a wall-stile ahead, and a thin trod crosses rough pasture to the left of the brow ahead. An improved path slants to the wall and up to a gate on the brow, looking down on Black Lane Ends. Descend the wallside to a gate into the Black Lane Ends pub car park (formerly Hare & Hounds).

Back in the field rise left to a wall-stile, and a path crosses to another. Crossing the dome of Piked Edge, Pendle Hill appears ahead. Drop to a stile in the far corner, and down a field centre to another, then a wall leads along to Harwes Farm. From a stile onto its drive, advance past the house and on a wallside cart track to a gate at the end. Advance a few strides to a gate on the right onto heathery Kelbrook Moor. Take the level left-hand path aiming for the top of a cluster of trees, then on again to a second, isolated clump. Stunning views look to a Bowland skyline between Pendle Hill and Ingleborough. Beyond the trees, a tiny moist section precedes a good path running to a gap in the wall ahead.

Through it the path resumes down Roger Moor, levelling out for a sustained contour before dropping again, sharply left as it then meanders down and right along to an outer wall corner. Pass right of it the short way further down to an inner corner with a ladder-stile off the moor. A faint path drops down to a small gate onto a farm road joining Cob Lane at Thick Bank. Turn down the road for a minute, then take a drive right past a house. Ignoring a gate into a field, an enclosed path runs outside the garden to a stile into a field. Drop to the wall heading away, using a stile in an early kink to resume on the other side of a tree-lined streamlet and fence, a grassy descent with the village below. The stream sinks below ground at the bottom: bear right to a gate/stile and descend past the re-born stream to a gate/stile in front of houses below. Bear left down the road to finish.

Pendle Hill from Kelbrook Moor

4³⁄4 miles from Foulridge

**Gentle, colourful hills
offering wide panoramas**

*Start Foulridge Wharf
(SD 888425; BB8 7PP), car park*
Map *OS Explorer OL21, South Pennines*

Foulridge village has pubs and shops, and the Wharf was an integral part of the Leeds-Liverpool Canal's heyday, here entering a mile-long tunnel. The surviving warehouse offers refreshments, while the moorings host a colourful array of boats. Head back on the access road, and meeting a through road go left on Towngate to a green. At the end climb steps to the A56 and cross to ascend Stoney Lane. At the top go right a few yards, then left up a corner of a tiny green. Just a few yards up this back road, take a snicket on the left between houses to a stile into a field. A path rises left, crossing to a small gate then on to another before crossing to a corner wall-stile. Cross to a gateway, then rise left past scattered rocks to a bridle-gate on the brow. Turn right to ascend with the wall, with a shapely knoll above. A thinner path forks left to contour on its left side across to a wall-stile. Through this ascend the wallside, meeting a further stile onto Noyna Hill's broad top.

As the wall moves away, an intervening stile is followed by a slight rise above a sparsely wooded bank. Reaching a wall-corner take a small gate on the right, and a path runs enclosed for 50 yards to a brow. Emerging, slant left down to a stile, then down to a corner gate onto Cob Lane at Noyna End. Opposite the house, a gate set back on the left sends a grassy track back across a field. Leave within 100 yards by dropping right to a footbridge on a streamlet. A path runs downstream towards a wall: don't use the gate ahead but turn steeply up the near side to a stile in the wall at the top. Continue rising with a fence up the extensive reedy tract of Great Edge, pausing to look back over Foulridge reservoirs, with Pendle Hill and Bowland's moors leading round to Yorkshire's Three Peaks. At the top veer right to a ladder-stile in the wall, and head away with a wall as far as a stile in it just short of its high point. Bear left across the field to a fence-stile, then advance past trees to a wall-stile. Bear left to a farm track, following it through a gate and across to a corner in front of Kelbrook Moor.

Don't enter but go left down the wallside to a corner gate into a walled way. Moist until opening out, stay with the right-hand wall down to an access road. Continue down past a shooting school and onto Cob Lane, going briefly left to an enclosed green way right. Entering a field, a grass track crosses to a bridle-gate, resuming above a wall to Ambwell. Pass the house and on to a bridle-gate at the end. Retain this course across a field, dropping steadily, through a gateway to a gate/stile just beyond. A little path traces the right-hand wall beneath a scrubby bank down to a gate/stile onto a drive, joining a road just below. Go briefly left to a gate on the right at a house, Cragg Farm. From a gate just beneath it, a stony track descends to the A56. From a gate/stile opposite slant right down the field, in the corner using a crossing of the old Colne-Skipton railway. A grassy way drops into a field, then advance to a footbridge ahead. A path rises to a canal bridge, where go left on the towpath the short way back to the start.

The canal at Foulridge Wharf

4$\frac{1}{4}$ miles from Wycoller

A fascinating exploration of Wycoller's little valley and its colourful flanks

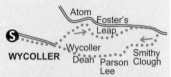

Start Car park (SD 926394; BB8 8SY), on approach road to hamlet
Map OS Explorer OL21, South Pennines

From the car park a path shadows the road into the absorbing hamlet of Wycoller. It is hard to believe that before the Industrial Revolution, several hundred people lived here, mostly handloom weaving. Having spent much of the 20th century largely derelict, its isolation and character have ensured its popularity at the heart of a country park. Central are the ruins of 16th century Wycoller Hall, reputedly the Ferndean Manor of Charlotte Bronte's 'Jane Eyre'. Alongside is an ancient clapper bridge, with a fine packhorse bridge by a ford. Restored Aisled Barn has information and Pepper Hill Barn has a study centre too. Refreshments are available. Cross the packhorse bridge to the hall and ascend steps up the grassy bank. At the top a broad, enclosed path rises away, with Pendle Hill seen back to the left. Adjacent upright slabs are a good example of vaccary walling - a vaccary was a cattle farm.

Higher, the path acquires a sunken section, and at a bend at the top take a bridle-gate on the right sending a path the short way up to the Atom Panopticon, a modern sculpture at Haworth Road car park. A path runs the few yards from it to the car park's right-hand end, then passes through an old wall to contour across the slope. Through another old wall it slants down to run to a kissing-gate in a wall. Big views look across Wycoller Dean to Boulsworth Hill, while just ahead are the boulders of Foster's Leap. Cross the field to another kissing-gate, and with the houses at Foster's Leap just beyond, fork left across the small field to a corner gate onto the drive. Rise steeply beneath a small wood as far as a hairpin bend left. Just yards higher, a grassy way contours right beneath the rocks of Foster's Leap. Remaining level it fades amid reeds, but with an old wall to the left beneath a steeper bank, the improved path rises steadily towards a house that appears ahead at Higher Key Styles: a wall-stile gives access. Cross a small enclosure to a gate on the right, then head out on the driveway up to Haworth Road.

Turn right for half a mile as the road traverses the edge of moorland. After the last house it swings sharply left on a brow, the walk's high point, with the Wolf Stones on the left skyline. Just a little further turn down an initially enclosed byway into the head of Smithy Clough. The well-surfaced road runs unfailingly down, crossing the stream by a stone-arched bridge amid the hummocks of Smithy Clough Scar, also known as Hilly Holes. These hushings result from centuries-old limestone extraction, where water released from dams scoured vegetation away. On swinging up to a brow, a gate/stile on the right send a broad, rougher way down between fence and new tree plantings to Parson Lee Farm at the bottom. Head away along its drive, merging with another at a confluence to resume as a traffic-free byway with the stream. This happy arrangement is maintained through Wycoller Dean back to the start, passing Copy House footbridge and the historic, single-slab Clam Bridge alongside a ford.

Wycoller Hall

4 miles from Trawden

Pick a clear day for this straightforward ascent of a supreme viewpoint

Start Hollin Hall (SD 915380; BB8 8TJ), roadside car park at Floats Mill on cul-de-sac half-mile south-east of church
Map *OS Explorer OL21, South Pennines*
Access *Open Access, dogs on leads*

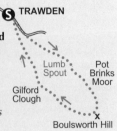

Trawden village has St Mary's church, the Trawden Arms, shop and cafe. The former mill at Hollin Hall is now residential. Leave by continuing along the road, bridging Trawden Brook to narrow into a country lane, climbing away then easing out, with Boulsworth Hill looking daunting ahead. At a sharp bend left go straight ahead on a drive to Lodge Moss Farm. Keep left of the main buildings to a bridle-gate at the far end. A grass track runs to a gate, then descends pleasantly to cross a tree-lined stream. A brief detour down the far bank finds a superb vantage point for the shady hollow enclosing the waterfall of Lumb Spout. Resuming, bear left up a distinct green way, fading as it eases out to cross to a gate/stile at a wall corner ahead. Continue up the wallside behind, rising gently to a stile onto an access road on the base of Pot Brinks Moor. Turn 50 yards right towards the barns at Spoutley Lumb, then left up a concrete access road to a covered reservoir.

A path takes over to commence the ascent proper. Beyond an early kissing-gate in a fence the good path enjoys a sustained steep section, which on easing reveals the summit further to the right. Gentler slopes lead up to Little Chair Stones, and the initially moist but later improving path bears right to slant up to the skyline Weather Stones. This is the best cluster on the walk, featuring some massive boulders. From here rolling moors stretch eastwards across the Pennine watershed to Crow Hill and Withins Height above the head of Walshaw Dean. A two-minute walk south-west across the broad top leads to the waiting Ordnance Survey column. Boulsworth Hill rises as an upturned boat from the rolling moorland, and its lengthy top bristles with gritstone outcrops. The summit, Lad Law, is itself a cluster of boulders, and at 1696ft/517m is one of the principal summits of the South Pennines. Panoramic views include the Yorkshire Dales, the Lake District and Bowland.

To commence the descent, take the main path heading west, aiming a little left of Pendle Hill. Initially moist in places, it passes above a peaty pool on a small shelf to drop to scattered boulders around the upright Abbot Stone. Here the ground steepens and the path becomes much drier. Almost levelling, it runs to a fence-stile to trace a wall (then fence) down through some moist moments to rejoin the rough road, now a cart track. Go left for 50 yards to a wall-stile by a gate on the right, from where a vague path heads down the left side of a broad tongue overlooking tree-lined Gilford Clough. Well before reaching a confluence, the clearer path slants left down to a footbridge on the stream, and up the other side to a small gate beneath Gilford Clough Farm. The path bears right outside the buildings to emerge onto the driveway. Advance along this, mirroring your outward route across the valley. Passing numerous houses you arrive at Meadow Bottom, where the access road drops onto the road at the start.

The summit of Boulsworth Hill

4¹₂ miles from Thursden

Magnificent views from good paths around enigmatic Thursden Valley: appreciable uphill work

Start *Broadbank Hill (SD 901351; BB10 3RB), car park 2 miles east of Haggate*

Map *OS Explorer OL21, South Pennines*

Thursden is a remote, scattered hamlet in a lovely side valley. Facing magnificent views to a moorland backdrop, turn left on the road, past a lone house to a T-junction beneath a wartime pillbox. Turn right to quickly reach a wood top, where a bridle-gate on the right sends a good track down through the trees. Easing out, it emerges onto a drive, going briefly left over Thursden Brook onto a minor road. Turn left for a short climb to cross a cattle grid to a junction, where a bridle-gate on the right sends a firm path rising between fence and wall to a pair of bridle-gates on Rieve Edge. The wall moves to your left as you rise onto Extwistle Moor.

Higher up you encounter small zigzags, levelling out to run to a gate at a wall corner. Resume with a fence to a path junction by a gate. Remain on the firm way bearing right to the walk's high point on a gentle brow, to then drop away above the valley of Swinden Water. When it drops more sharply left at a junction take the level track right, improving to contour around to a gate in a wall. Remain on the inviting level track straight ahead, later dropping gently beneath old quarry spoil to a gateway in an old wall, where Swinden Reservoir appears ahead. Here your way fades: bear gently left over rolling pasture, picking up a grass track from the right to contour faintly along to a small gate in a wall.

A good little path contours away along the base of steeper slopes overlooking the reservoir. At the end above a lower dam, a stile by a pylon puts you onto a track. Cross and bear briefly right to a wallside grass track through a gate/stile in a fence ahead. This green way rises marginally before contouring around with the wall into the side valley of Holden Clough. It drops to a moist dip, then leaves the wall by slanting right, rising gently between old walls to a gate/stile. A continuation rises more steeply by a wall to a gate/stile at the top into the grounds of Sweetwell kennels. Rise away up the access road to open out at a fork on the brow. Go left here, and as it swings left downhill take a stile in the wall ahead.

Head away to a line of quarry spoil at the end, overlooking Park Wood and the Thursden scene. A super path slants right down above the wood, and just short of the corner it drops left between the trees, shortly taking a kissing-gate in the fence on your right. The path then runs upstream with Thursden Brook, out of the trees to a footbridge. Across it take a stile just in front, and rise briefly steeply up the scrubby slope to an outbuilding. Through the gate to its right take a stile just above, then ascend a field with a fence on your right. At Stephen Hey Farm, waymarks encourage you left outside the grounds to a gate just behind, joining the drive just before joining a minor road. Rise left 75 yards to a stile on the right, and bear right across a large, sloping pasture. Initially rising only slightly, as you reach a lone hawthorn make a steeper slant to the top of a stand of hawthorns: just a little higher is a fence-stile back into the car park.

Thursden Valley from Park Wood

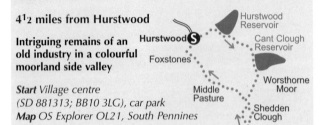

4¹₂ miles from Hurstwood

Intriguing remains of an old industry in a colourful moorland side valley

Start Village centre
(SD 881313; BB10 3LG), car park
Map OS Explorer OL21, South Pennines

Hurstwood is a charming hamlet, with Hurstwood Hall amid several venerable old houses. From the centre by the phonebox and bridge, turn right up the lane with the stream, passing the modest church. Quickly ending at the last house, advance straight on an inviting green way into an open area. The main path rises left with a wall to the top of the bank, and along to a kissing-gate into trees. The path ascends the wood edge to a sharp turn left, where take a stile in front to follow a path rising the short way through trees to a footbridge over the outflow of Hurstwood Reservoir. Across it the path joins the embankment and follows it right to the far end. Across the reservoir are bleak moors, with the first evidence of the 'hushings' that are a major feature of the walk. These are the scars of centuries-old limestone extraction workings.

At the end you pass through a gate to join a firm access road, going left through a gate over a drain onto open moor. Take the right fork, which itself rapidly forks as you rise away: either will suffice as they quickly merge again. Coal Clough windfarm is seen just to the right. Rising to a brow, a grassy sward reveals Cant Clough Reservoir ahead, and the track drops to an access road at the dam. Cross the dam to a gate onto grassy Worsthorne Moor, and remain on the track, swinging right with a fence. Big views look back over Burnley to the Bowland moors and round to Pendle Hill. The way meanders pleasantly along to drop gently to cross a stone-arched bridge on the stream in Shedden Clough. You shall return to this point after the 'sheddings loop'.

Remain on the track on the far bank, re-crossing at a ford. Continue with a wall past information panels, with rashes of stones from hushings to your left. Soon reaching a footbridge/ford by a stone enclosure, cross and remain on the track rising away to become enclosed. A grassy section precedes reaching trees on your left. As it swings sharp left at a corner where the left-hand wall ends, take a path right through a gateway. A level stroll, initially with a wall, runs beneath a new wood, then drops gently to another panel on a rhododendron-draped knoll: a good viewpoint for myriad hummocks of the old workings. The path drops down a groove to its left, emerging from bushes to pass a limekiln amid further stony rashes. The path then swings right out of the site to rejoin the earlier path above the ford/footbridge. Retrace steps back to the stone bridge.

Don't cross but take the kissing-gate in front, and a path rises between new plantings and on to a gate into a field. The way runs to a gate/stile to meet a harder track, and on above Middle Pasture Farm. A setted section drops down a large pasture, over a cattle-grid and past another farm to a cluster of houses at Foxstones. After advancing a few yards to admire Foxstones Farm set back on the right, drop down the near side of the nearest house, Rose Cottage. The 'road' is quickly replaced by a footway down to a wooded bank, where it slants down to stone-arched Foxstones Bridge. Up the other side you emerge back in the hamlet alongside 16th century Spenser's House.

Hushings at Shedden Clough

4½ miles from Holme Chapel

Good paths in the Cliviger Gorge

Start Ratten Clough (SD 890269; OL14 8QT), large layby on sidelined section of A646, 1½ miles south-east

Map *OS Explorer OL21, South Pennines*

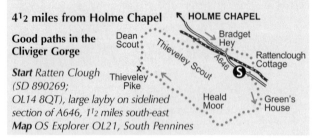

From the Todmorden end of the car park, cross dramatic Ratten Clough to a stile opposite Rattenclough Cottage. A good path slants up through trees, and out at the top to maintain its slant outside the wood. At the top corner cross a streamlet to a fence-stile ahead, from where resume pathless between old wall and fence. Quickly easing, advance to a bridle-gate in the fence above Green's House. Big views look down into Cornholme backed by Stoodley Pike, with Coal Clough windfarm across the valley. A grass track heads away, curving round above Beater Clough, the county boundary. As it shortly swings left on crossing a streamlet, rise right to an old wall and fence-stile. A grassy path rises left across grassy Heald Moor, a very gentle climb to suddenly gain the crest.

While a path advances straight on, take that branching right to tramp the very broad ridge for the ensuing mile, parts of which can be moist after wet weather. Crossing a farm track in a very slight dip, the improving path meets an old wall rising from the left. The path rises with it to a gate at a wall junction to resume across open moor. With the Ordnance Survey column on Thieveley Pike appearing, you pass a stone Limers Gate waymarker. Meeting a fence/wall a little further, cross the stile and go a few yards left to the 1473ft/449m summit, a former beacon site with an excellent panorama. Leave by a grassy path bearing right, declining steadily to cross a level grass track. Just below is a fence/wall corner above a massive, scooped hollow: here the path forks, soon to rejoin.

The right one traces the fence over a knoll to drop more steeply above the hollow: easily missed over the fence as you descend are shapely Dean Scout rocks. Re-united at a bridle-gate at the bottom, a gateway on the right sends a path away with an old wall/fence, and a wooded hollow on your right. Soon dropping to a fork at a clearing and old wall junction, the crags of Thieveley Scout take shape above. Keep straight on between young trees with a wall on your right, at the end crossing a streamlet to leave the wood at a gate ahead. A faint grass track crosses open pasture, joined by an old wall to reach an old wall corner. Here the track slants left through the wall and down above a stand of trees, doubling back beneath them to a rail underpass beneath a mast. Emerging onto a rough access road, go right up to the main road.

Cross to the footway and go right to a rail bridge. While the start is just five minutes further, avoid the road by turning left up the short drive to Bradget Hey. Bear right here over a cattle-grid and along a rough access road through two fields to New Hey Farm. Remain on the track left of the buildings to the left-hand gate at the end. A grass track heads away, but leave by a gate on the right before the end. Descend with an old wall to your right, and in the bottom corner go right to the railway. With kissing-gates either side, cross to a grassy way running to a gate/stile to rejoin the road by Rattenclough Cottage.

Cliviger from Dean Scout

3½ miles from Crown Point

Good paths and big views visiting a modern moorland landmark

Start Crown Point (SD 847288; BB11 3RL), Singing Ringing Tree Panopticon car park
Map *OS Explorer OL21, South Pennines*

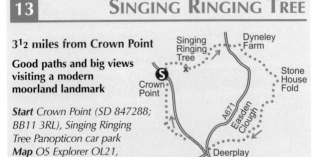

From the isolated car park it is a few minutes' walk along a firm path to the Singing Ringing Tree. One of a number of large-scale sculptures in open-air East Lancashire settings, it comprises of steel pipes through which the wind makes remarkable, eerie noises. From a stile in the adjacent fence, a thin path heads away towards a corner just ahead, where turn down the near side of the wall. The faint and sometimes moist path descends rough pasture alongside reeds to a stile in a gateway at the bottom. Continue down more pleasantly on lush grass with an old wall to your left, at the bottom dropping right to a stile/gate at isolated Leads Cottage. Descend the steep drive through colourful terrain onto the A671 at Heyne Farm, a former inn.

Cross to the footway and go 50 yards right to a stile/steps down into a field. Go right over the tree-lined streamlet of Buck Clough and turn down its side, dropping to a stile at the bottom onto a rough access road with Dyneley Farm ahead. Turn sharp right on its enclosed course beneath a steeper bank to ultimately arrive at Stone House Fold. Pass between the two houses to a gate ahead, then leave the track by rising to a gate to your right. A good track rises away with a fence, soon swinging right up towards an outer fence corner. Keeping left here, it transforms into a lush green way, rising steeply with a ditch and hedge to your right. At the top corner you arrive at a striking memorial to Lady Mary

Towneley, an indefatigable horsewoman who was instrumental in improving Pennine bridleways. Through the gate you join a rough track, rising to a cattle-grid into open pasture. As it quickly swings up to the left, bear right on a more inviting grassy track. The deep valley of Easden Clough to your right is overlooked by a tip at a former quarry. Crossing the big pasture, the track drops to a reedy streamlet and rises to join Cow Side farm road. Go right on its lush verge, rising at the end to a gate back onto the A671.

Turn left up the road to quickly reach a junction with the B6238 Rawtenstall road at the site of Deerplay Toll Bar. Here double back right up unsigned Crown Point Road, rising to soon reach a rough road going left. Go briefly up here, and from a stile on the right before reaching a gate, a firm path heads away. This runs a splendid course, largely level as it winds around through scattered new plantings, later absorbing a path from the left before running through moderately denser pine trees. Emerging onto a brow with open views, a fence comes in to guide the path past tapering trees to run parallel with the road. A little further a stile puts you onto the road at a cattle-grid on the brow, past which the start point is just 100 yards further. *At the Singing Ringing Tree*

GREAT HAMELDON

4¼ miles from Hapton

Much of interest around this lofty landmark hovering above Burnley

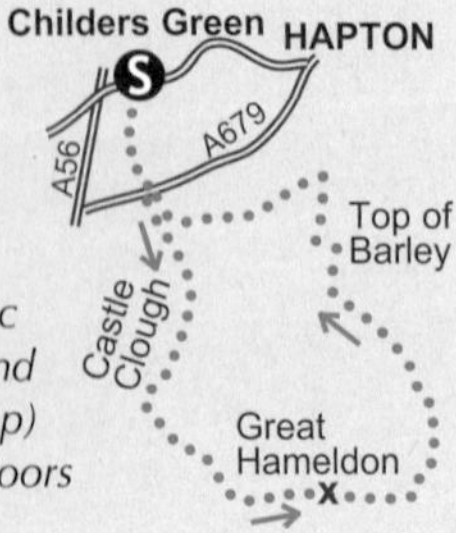

Childers Green HAPTON

Start *Childers Green (SD 784307; BB11 5QX), small laybys at Mill Hill picnic area on Mill Hill Lane between Hapton and Huncoat (doesn't merit 'P' symbol on map)*
Map *OS Explorer 287, West Pennine Moors*
Access *Open access, not grouse moors*

At the hamlet's eastern end and the small common's western end, a grassy path heads south, descending outside house grounds into trees and through a stile to a footbridge. Just beyond, it emerges to scale a scrubby bank to a kissing-gate into a meadow. The path heads away, veering left between sheds to a stile onto a driveway at the A679. Cross to a parking area and kissing-gate into Hameldon Woods, and a broad path rises away. Quickly meeting a broader way turn left, rising to ultimately swing right to a bridle-gate out at the top. A broad path rises away beneath spoil of the former Hameldon Quarries. Quickly meeting a level path turn right, winding around and swinging left up to an early junction with a broader path. Turn right, around past a small knoll to another junction beneath steep, rough flanks. Bear right on a path running an undulating course beneath heathery slopes. At a fork after a reedy streamlet, keep right to run above a wall enclosing trees, at the end reaching a fence in front of colourful Castle Clough.

Rise gently left above the fence to find a path quickly forming, running on to approach an apparent impasse. Keep right until beneath the crags, then the path rises steeply and roughly left to soon emerge onto easy ground at the top. Joining a level path, turn right around the valley head to a path junction at an old wall. Take a thin path rising left with the wall to quickly level out: Great Hameldon's domed top appears above. The path forges on through bleak surrounds, arriving at a fence-stile at a path junction with a gate on the right. Here take the path rising left with the fence, and as it quickly turns off, cross a moist area on this improving path rising to the skyline. A steep little finale finds Great Hameldon's Ordnance Survey column just in front. At 1342ft/409m it boasts a massive panorama, including Bowland and the Yorkshire Dales.

Of several vague departing paths, head east for the masts on nearby Hameldon Hill. After an initially moist 30 yards it transforms into a good trod, soon dropping gently through intermittent moist moments to meet a firm path by a crumbling wall. Turn left, initially with large slabs in a groove, improving as Thorny Bank Clough opens steeply below. The path now commences a long, gentle curve beneath spoil heaps, later joined by a track from the left to drop down above Thorney Bank. Absorbing its drive it curves down to the sprawling farm at Top of Barley. Here take a rough track left, but when it swings sharp left, turn right on an embanked path on the course of a quarry tramway, passing a ruin to drop gently to a grassy wallside track at the bottom. Go left to a kissing-gate into another tract of Hameldon Woods, and a well-made, level path heads away to end above a ditch. Turn briefly right to a lesser ditch, across which drop left to a footbridge and on to a stile out of the wood. Head away to a derelict house, passing right of the buildings and out on the drive down to the A679. Cross to retrace opening steps.

Looking over Castle Clough

33

15   UPPER RIVER IRWELL

4½ miles from Bacup

**A rich variety of ways
around the upper reaches
of the youthful River Irwell**

Start Town centre (SD 868230;
OL13 9AE), car parks
Map OS Explorer OL21,
South Pennines

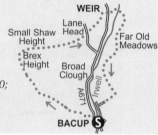

From the central roundabout head north on the A671 Burnley Road, passing churches on each side. A little further turn left up suburban Ash Street: ending abruptly at the top, bear right up a rough track. Soon swinging left uphill, it becomes a nicer green way, later bending right to end at a kissing-gate. Five scruffy minutes follow: cross to a stile at a fence corner just ahead, then rise with the fence to a gate. Continue up the improving pasture with a sunken section to gates at the top. From the central one go a few yards with the wall on your right, then bear left up the slope, a line of reeds pointing to an old wall. When this fades advance a little further, and with a fence to your right, continue to the brow where a grass track comes in from the left to reach a kissing-gate by the left-hand gate.

Through this advance along a super grassy track, with rough moorland over the fence and big views left. This remains your level course for a substantial time. Passing through three gates the way fades: rise slightly alongside a brief walled section, then on between pools to cross to an old wall/fence and ruin ahead. Turn right on the near side to a corner stile/gate, and continue with the fence on your right, rising along two field edges with an intervening stile. A stile at the top corner puts you onto the adjacent moor of Brex Height. Go briefly left to a stile back out, then advance to a fence-stile ahead.

Slant left down the pasture to a corner stile, and drop away with a sturdy wall. Through a stile at the bottom corner, continue to slant across the reedy pasture, crossing a fence near the bottom

34

corner and along to a corner wall-stile/gate after bridging a streamlet above a colourful ravine. Heading away, quickly bear right down to a stile, and a path drops the short way to another onto a lane above Lane Head Farm. From a wall-stile opposite, head away with an old wall slanting down a fieldside, through a corner stile and down again to another. Now drop the very short way to a near hidden stile in a wall sending an enclosed path rising left. Emerging via a stile at the end, go on through two enclosures to a stile onto an access road. Turn right down to the A671 at Weir, with a cafe up to the left.

Across, go down Weir Lane to the end of houses at the bottom. Between two older ones on the left is a bridge on the River Irwell, and a few yards further a surfaced path rises away. Levelling out, it winds round above a waterfall (viewed just after the bridge) and up to a house at Scar End. Advance on the drive, and when it drops away take a cart track through a gate ahead. Dropping to Far Old Meadows, pass through the hamlet, and at a junction where it drops right, take the access track ahead. This remains your course for a lengthy time, passing several houses then narrowing to a footway after the last one. It continues beneath an arch from a former colliery before emerging into an open area. Advance to the Sentinel cairn on the Irwell Sculpture Trail. Here drop right on a broad path outside housing, becoming an access road onto a road. Drop between a school and football ground, turning left at the bottom, and a little further dropping right back to the centre.

Colliery arch

3¾ miles from Calderbrook

Splendid grassy moorland ways

*Start Church (SD 941181; OL15 9NW),
parking on Calderbrook Road, off
A6033 a mile north of Littleborough*
Map *OS Explorer OL21,
South Pennines*
Access *Open Access, not grouse moors*

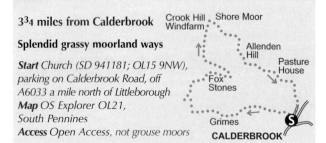

Take the side road of Higher Calderbrook Road ascending
steeply right of St James's church, quickly taking a rough road left.
Rising onto open moor, it swings left beneath colourful slopes, and
at a gate runs enclosed to Grimes. Through a gate behind the buildings
you re-enter moorland, and ignoring a track right, advance a
minute further to the next fork. Take an inviting grassy way slanting
right, with Crook Hill windfarm appearing above. This rises to merge
with the track from the gate to run a splendid course, curving up
and around the slopes of Ringing Pots Hill. Levelling out, it runs
grandly along with the valley of Blue Pot Brook down to your left.

Ignoring a lesser cross-track you quickly reach the clough,
crossing an embankment to rise steadily out the other side. The
track runs to a wall junction ahead, but leave 35 yards before it on
a faint trod doubling back right. This runs above the track you just
left, crossing a broad, ascending path above the embankment. A
tenuous trod continues towards the clough, and nearing it curves
gently left to run through bracken above the rim. Becoming
slightly clearer, it quickly approaches a confluence. Cross to a trod
running a few yards upstream to the confluence, where the bracken
ends and there's no obvious onward way. Rise away right, quickly
easing to reveal an old wall not far above. Rising towards it, the
trod is resurrected amid bracken to cross a distinct reedy channel
and a groove just prior to gaining an outer corner of the wall. A
grass track immediately before the wall will be put to use fairly shortly.

Go left on a thin trod with the wall, running a pleasant course as it swings right beneath a slope, then under the bouldery edge of Fox Stones from which some rocks fall to your path. At the end you rise to the ruin of Forest Lodge, a former gamekeeper's lodge. With scattered boulders above, take a thin path rising left above a smaller ruin just beyond: within yards you arrive on a shelf beneath further boulders. Take the path left, curving around through boulders and rising very gently above the steeper slope that you've just passed beneath. The path leaves the rocks to run on to arrive above the wall's second bend. As you start to drop left to the grassy track from earlier, take a lesser right fork to cross the short way to the track. Turn right for a superb, gentle rise across the moor bound for the windfarm, ultimately meeting its service road.

Go right, and 150 yards before the penultimate turbine, a small cairn on the right sends a little path down onto the moor. Quickly levelling out, keep left at a fork to reach an abrupt brow on Allenden Hill overlooking steep slopes. Turn right on a splendid continuation, curving down above the rim to cross to a gate off the moor. A grass track runs the length of an enclosure and on to Pasture House. To its right, join the drive dropping past further houses to a back road. Go right, past cottages at Higher Calderbrook to absorb your outward route for the final yards.

At Forest Lodge

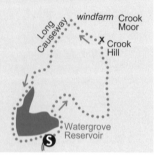

4½ miles from Wardle

Superb moorland paths high above a popular reservoir

Start *Watergrove Reservoir (SD 911176; OL12 9NJ), water company car park north of village*
Map *OS Explorer OL21, South Pennines*

Watergrove Reservoir was completed in 1938, flooding the hamlet from which it is named. From the car park follow the access road rising to the right end of the dam, and go left outside the reservoir wall incorporating old dated lintels. The reservoir is surrounded by moors, with the shapely pairing of Brown Wardle Hill and Middle Hill across the water and Crook Hill windfarm above. An early bridle-gate in the wall sends a nicer path along the shore as far as a kissing-gate where you opt to rejoin the rough road. Cross straight over to a firm bridleway rising through a memorial wood. Quickly reaching a gate at the top onto grassy moorland, follow this good track uphill, then swinging right to a gate in a sturdy wall. Through it the track runs a level wallside course to reach a fence-gate where the wall parts company.

Advance just a minute further, and after passing a small marshy area beneath spoil heaps from old coal workings, leave the track for an invisible right of way to the left. This simply involves slanting gently right up the easy turf, within minutes meeting a broad pathway. Go left on this for a sustained, foolproof rise across the moor: the reservoir makes an appearance part way up, while a distinctive stone shelter occupies the skyline far ahead in front of the windfarm. Your path gains the gentle ridge to look down on Turn Slack Dam on your right, then continues the short way up to finally arrive at the circular shelter on the brow.

The path continues away, still aiming for the turbines to rise very gently to a cairn at 1338ft/408m on Crook Hill, the summit of Crook Moor. With the turbines just behind, the continuing path bears left to slowly descend the crest, with the site's service road just over to your right. The path declines to a gentle dip where a major cross-paths is marked by a standing stone. Here you join the Long Causeway, a packhorse route over the moors to Todmorden. Turn left down this with the reservoir ahead, crossing a level path and descending on modern flagstones. Part way down you meet a track that served coal pits on your left, with further remains to your right. Continue down to meet a firm track at a gate off the moor.

Pass through and follow this away between old walls, with a length of stone causey once used by quarrymen's carts. At an open area with stone setts, take a branch right through a gate. Quickly dropping to a gate into the trees of Higher Slack Brook nature reserve, the track then runs left with the stream to a footbridge over it. Ignore this and resume the short way further into trees to pass left of a pond and join the popular reservoir circuit path. Turn right on this, bridging the beck and running a very pleasant course, emerging from trees and remaining near the shore to meet a water company road at the end. Cross this and the outflow bridge, and conclude by going left on the embankment to a flight of steps down to the car park. *The Long Causeway*

4½ miles from Broadley

A popular and fascinating river gorge beneath the moors

Start Healey Dell (SD 880162; OL12 6LW), parking either side of road bridge at end of suburbia on Station Road off A671
Map OS Explorer OL21, South Pennines

From the near side of the road bridge, take an initially steep path left signed to Fairy Chapel. Entering the wooded valley, an early cul-de-sac branch right descends steep steps to a viewing platform for the River Spodden's fine ravine. The main path continues slanting beneath a quarried face to a sharp bend above waterfalls, then swings right to ruinous Th'Owd Mill i'th Thrutch, with its little bridge. With Healey Dell Viaduct ahead, the path rises beneath it to a narrow road. Drop right to Healey Dell Cottages, and down a snicket outside the gardens to a footbridge on the Spodden. Across, the path goes briefly left to commence a sustained slant right up Smallshaw Wood, bridging the brook to emerge and ascend a field edge to Smallshaw Farm. Through the gate at the top go left on a short green way into the yard: the house bears a 1622 datestone. The setted access road leads out past a pond to Catley Lane Head.

Turn right over a cattle-grid where the surface ends, and rise away up initially setted Rooley Moor Road. After a cross-ways it rises more roughly through a gate, and up the moor ignoring a branch forking left. When a level branch goes left, advance 100 yards further to a rougher track right. Instantly becoming a fine grassy way, it features a section of causey used by quarrymen's carts. Spring Mill Reservoir is down to the right. Beneath the boulders of Cat Stones you absorb the course of a tramway that served Bagden Quarry. Nearing a wall the track swings left, but cross the start of a reedy ditch to a fence-stile ahead. The path continues along an embankment, at the end passing through an old wall and then a gate in a sturdy wall. The path runs a further 100 yards to a ruin overlooking tree-lined Fern Isle Brook, and 100 yards further to the extensive, long-abandoned Bagden Quarry.

Without entering, double back right down a grassy groove onto gentler ground, and bear right. A little path runs to a kissing-gate in a fence above the deep clough, improving to run on to the start of a mercurial grassy way curving down the steep flank. With Spring Mill Reservoir ahead, it drops to a footbridge. Across it a path puts you on another old way, turning right to rise to a wall at a stile/gate. Continuing with the wall to Houses o' th' Hill, follow the cart track left behind the buildings to drop to buildings at Fold Head. At the end it swings sharp right down through more houses, becoming surfaced to join a road in front of a school on the edge of Whitworth. Go right to a junction on a sharp bend, and briefly right past a former millpond. Here turn down a path to a junction, and go right through trees to meet a suburban street. A few yards further, go left over a rail bridge to a firm path slanting right down onto the old line. Advance along this amid greenery to a clearing, and through the gate ahead passing Broadley Stone Siding into a wooded cutting. When the road bridge appears ahead at Broadley station platform, take a broad branch left up to the road at the bridge.

The River Spodden in Healey Dell

3¹₂ miles from Waterfoot

An absorbing circuit of a rounded hill with intriguing quarry remains

Start Town centre (SD 833218; BB4 7EU), car parks
Map OS Explorer OL21, South Pennines

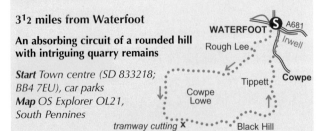

From the mini roundabout head briefly west on the A681, and after bridging the River Irwell turn left on Duke Street. At the end go left to a turning circle, across which a path rises right through a bridle-gate above the river's steep bank. The path quickly swings right for a sustained slant up through a beechwood. At the top it runs right above the wood, avoiding marshy moments and on to the wood end. Don't use the gateway in front, but turn left up the fenceside to a gate onto an access road at the hamlet of Rough Lee. Go briefly right to the next house, then double back left on a cart track to a stile alongside Manor House. Ascend the steep, pathless field with massive views over the valley. At a solitary tree an old wall points the way up to a stile in a wall above. With Cowpe Lowe's rounded top above, rise up this large field to a stile at the top right corner. Rising a few yards, ignore an ascending path and go right to cross a streamlet at the scant ruins of Lowe End.

A modest path runs on with an old wall, and when this drops away, advance a little further to join a grassy track coming up from the right. This now leads on for a while to a gentle brow. Dropping slightly to an outer wall corner, it becomes stony as it runs on near the wall. Either cross the drain on your left and go directly to a gateway ahead at an outer wall corner, or remain on the track to the corner ahead, then left to the gateway. Through the wall bear left up to the embankment of a dam. Pass along its right side, and a short way further to meet a track in front of quarry spoil. This is the course of a 19th century tramway that took stone down from Cragg and Ding Quarries. Go left, passing further quarry spoil, with Scout Moor windfarm ahead. Rising very slightly and ignoring a right branch, the track features a distinct embanked section, becoming almost level as it curves left up to a kissing-gate in front of a deep tramway cutting. Just ahead, your path joins a firm track. Go ahead on this alongside the cutting, now with stone flags worn by quarrymen's carts around the rear of Cowpe Lowe. Over to your right the windfarm hovers above a small reservoir.

With a wall to your right, the path runs to a fork. Prefer the higher one which curves round an embankment to re-unite at a guidepost in front of heathery Black Hill. Here turn left down a fenceside track to a gate off the moor. Continue on the track down a large pasture, levelling to reveal Cowpe Reservoir ahead. Resuming downhill, it becomes steeper and stony down to a hairpin bend. Go straight ahead to successive gates to pass along the rear of Tippett. On the drive alongside, a stile on the left by an outhouse sends a flagged path down a scrubby enclosure to a stile. Negotiating a miry tract, drop by the wall then take a stile on the left just before the bottom. Joining an access road, turn down it to a cattle-grid then across a field to run beneath a pond. At a gate onto a surfaced access road, go right beneath a larger pond, becoming setted and passing a car park to join Cowpe Road. Drop back into the centre, bridging the Irwell to finish.

Cribden from under Cowpe Low

4½ miles from Haslingden

A Rossendale landmark high above numerous other features

Start Town centre (SD 785232; BB4 5QN), car parks
Map OS Explorer 287, West Pennine Moors

From the central crossroads head north on Deardengate, lined with shops and ending at a setted square. Cross the road and head away on Church Street. Rising past St James's church you quickly reach a junction at Rake Foot. Keep right on the main road, briefly, then at houses at Rock Hall go left on their drive and the continuing enclosed cart track rising away. On the brow, just before rejoining the road, take a stile on the left. From another behind, a path slants right, rising to a kissing-gate onto Cribden End Lane. Go right to a fork by the Halo car park at Top of Slate.

You shall return to this point after your walk over Cribden, so for now fork left on Watery Lane to a brow just above, where the road ends and becomes a gently descending byway with Cribden's slopes to the right. A sharper drop leads to the start of its 'watery' section, where packhorses would tramp the ditch with their leaders ('jaggers') on the dry embankment. Across the streamlet, follow this tidy section to the end. Resuming as a rough road to a crossroads of ways, go straight across on Laund Lane. A minute further, take a gate on the right at Greenhouse Farm, a forest school, and head directly away on a waymarked straight line. Go briefly on the drive to a stile ahead, up an access track, up and over a driveway and up a short drive to the next stile alongside a horse yard. Up a small pasture to a stile out of the grounds, take an immediate one on the right. Rising between fences into an unkempt area, rise left to join a track up to a ruin beneath Cribden's heathery slopes.

Behind the ruin a path runs left above the wall/fence, through a bridle-gate at the end then across to a stile/gate as the wall below returns. A track drops the short way to Brow Edge, but remain outside at a small gate ahead. Over a wall-stile beyond, resume across a pasture to arrive above Further Houses. Ignoring a wall-stile in front, rise right above a streamlet to a wall-corner stile. A trod rises with the wall onto Cribden Moor, with a fence-stile at the top where the wall turns off. Advance briefly with the fence to the brow, and slightly further to a stile on the right. The path heading away with an old wall/fence will lead ultimately to Cribden's top. When the wall turns off, a kissing-gate in the fence sees a good little path rise gently alongside, meeting an intervening stile and two kissing-gates to gain the featureless summit at 1315ft/401m.

Depart by dropping marginally and on to a kissing-gate on Cribden End, where the ground falls steeply away. Drop right to the bottom corner, meeting a level path at a gate. Through it turn left on a clear path along two fieldsides to a stile onto Watery Lane just above the Halo car park. Take a track rising from the car park to the monumental 2007 sculpture, then resume on the firm path on its other side, passing viewpoint seats to a T-junction. Go right to another junction, then left a few yards to an outer wall corner. Go left at this fork, dropping through woodland then swinging right, parallel with the road into more open surrounds. Meeting another path, drop left to a kissing-gate back onto Cribden End Lane. Go right as it winds down as Higher Lane to re-enter town, keeping left to the junction with Church Street.

The Halo

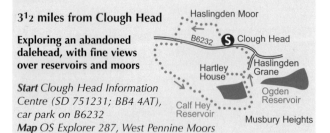

3¹₂ miles from Clough Head

Exploring an abandoned dalehead, with fine views over reservoirs and moors

Start *Clough Head Information Centre (SD 751231; BB4 4AT), car park on B6232*
Map *OS Explorer 287, West Pennine Moors*

The hugely popular information centre with refreshments tells the story of the abandoned valley of Haslingden Grane. A concession path leaves a kissing-gate left of the centre, climbing a wooded bank to another such gate, then steeply up a wallside to meet the Rossendale Way. Turn left through a kissing-gate and shadow the wall gently rising away beneath Haslingden Moor's grassy slopes, overtopped by a section of the Hyndburn windfarm. Levelling out, after passing a small plantation a fence-stile is met. Cross and descend the lush pasture, veering to the right of a fence corner to a stile onto the B6232. Cross to the verge and go left 100 yards to a cart track heading away.

Beyond a stile/gate it swings right and runs dead-straight until fading before a wall corner. A continuing path swings left across an open slope, with Calf Hey Reservoir over to the left. The thin path advances on, dropping gently with a deep, reedy way to a crumbling wall at the bottom. Down between scant old walls in a dip, an old walled way rises opposite, but leave almost at once through a gap on the left. A flagged section features before the fainter path contours across to an evocative ruin at Close Bottom. With Ogden Reservoir now also visible ahead, cross a drain to reach another ruin. The clearer path runs within old walls to the more substantial ruins at Top o' th' Knoll, passing to their right and down to cross a stream. The path rises behind to a gate into a plantation, then runs a level course to a small quarry site and NFPS sign.

The path drops delightfully into a clearing with views to Musbury Height's colourful flanks south of the reservoir, then slants left into denser trees. Through a scant wall it runs the short way left to a broad, firm path. Go right, quickly over a footbridge, and the upper path heading away runs on to soon reach a footbridge at the foot of Hog Lowe Clough. Cross and rise right a few yards to a fork, where keep left on the main contouring path across open terrain beneath trees. With Calf Hey Reservoir now just below, it runs to a kissing-gate and footbridge into open country beneath heathery flanks.

Stay on the path until almost above the dam, and the second NFPS sign in five minutes, by a lone sycamore, sends a path down to a stile onto a road. Cross the dam, with Ogden Reservoir below, and at the end keep left on a path rising to a kissing-gate onto an access road. While your onward route is straight up, first go briefly left to see the remains of Hartley House, with an informative panel. Retrace the road back to rise the short way to Calf Hey car park at the old hamlet of Haslingden Grane. At the end, above a burial ground, a small gate sends a path left above trees to avoid the road, rejoining it a little higher. Without setting foot on it take a path left, rising along a wood edge to a kissing-gate and then on through trees. At the end it arrives next to the B6232, and runs left to a kissing-gate onto it. Go briefly left on the verge, then cross to a gap sending a path through trees back to the start. *Calf Hey Reservoir*

47

4 miles from Helmshore

A magnificent excursion on excellent paths encircling a deep clough in moorland folds

Start Helmshore Museum (SD 778214; BB4 4NP), car park on B2635

Map OS Explorer 287, West Pennine Moors

Musbury Heights

HELMSHORE

S

B6235

Musbury Clough

Tor Hill · Tor End

Great House

Musden Head Moor

Helmshore Mills Textile Museum is an absorbing attraction with cafe/shop. At the end of the car park a firm path bears right across grass to a gate onto an enclosed path, going right over the River Ogden onto the main road opposite Park Mill. Cross and turn left, and after a row of cottages go right on Park Road. Keep right as it bridges Musbury Brook, rising as a rough lane by a row of houses. At the end turn sharp left after a car park along a rough road, with Tor Hill (Musbury Tor) rising to your left. Re-crossing the brook to houses at Carr Lane, to their right the track bridges the stream to quickly end. From a gate/stile on the left, a path briefly shadows the brook to a gate/stile onto a parallel green track.

Rising at the end to a gate/stile, it climbs right outside wooded Hare Clough, with a gate midway. A little further up it swings left, rising between old walls to the scant remains of Hare Clough. The unkempt track doubles sharply back, and as it swings up left, keep straight on with the fence on your right to an early stile in it. Across, head away amid new plantings to join an old wall curving to a crumbling wall-corner at Hare Clough. Crossing to a bridle-gate, a path rises away above a ditch, past an old wall and onto gentler ground, running to a wall corner above. Just yards along the wallside a stile is met, with Musbury Heights Quarry behind.

Without using the stile a path strikes left to commence a near-level traverse around the head of Musbury Clough. Quickly reaching the old farm of Rushy Leach, continue with odd moist moments as you shadow a drain. When it slants downhill, advance on to the ruin of Bailiff's Rake. Through a gateway behind, drop down with a wall on the right, through a fence gateway then lower down through a gateway in the wall near the bottom to cross a stream. The path rises to another gateway, behind which is the next ruin, Musden Head. After this you encounter the twin feeders of Musbury Brook beneath steeper slopes. Re-emerging you head away to arrive above another ruin. The path now leaves this valley and angles gently up with an old wall onto a brow. Crossing left to an outer wall corner, it runs left between fence and wall to a gate into a field on your right at the tame rear of Musbury Tor.

Resume diagonally across the field to a gate/stile in a wall, where a track forms to run past trees to a corner gate: a concrete track drops to a farm at Great House. Don't enter but take a faint wallside way left beneath the Tor's steep slopes. Through a stile at the end continue to another, then right down the wallside through fence-stiles onto an access road by a house. Go briefly left on it to a setted yard at Tor End, but don't enter. Instead take a wall-stile on your left sending a wallside path away. Through a stile drop again with a wall, and when it turns off advance to a steep drop with a bird's-eye view over the start. Drop down with a fence on your left to the old track of Musbury Road, and right through a kissing-gate to descend its setted course back onto Park Road. *Musbury Tor*

4³⁄₄ miles from Holcombe

Easy moorland walking through splendid scenery, dominated by the landmark Peel Tower

Start *Peel Tower car park
(SD 781162; BL8 4NN), on B6214
(Lumb Carr Road) above Ramsbottom*
Map *OS Explorer 287,
West Pennine Moors*

The settlement of Holcombe sits at the base of Holcombe Moor, overlooked by the mighty Peel Tower. Cross the road to an enclosed path rising onto setted Cross Lane. Turn right to where the setts end, then double back left on a rough access road onto the foot of the moor. Almost at once branch right, which after an initial bend makes a sustained slant left across the flank of the steep, colourful moor. Remain on this with its big views over the Irwell Valley. At the top the track turns right and eases to approach Top o' th' Moor Farm. Here take a path right up to a seat, then rising pleasantly across colourful terrain to the waiting tower. Over 120ft/36m high, it was built in 1851 to commemorate Sir Robert Peel. Born in Bury in 1788, as Prime Minister he is known as the founder of the modern police force, hence the nicknames 'bobbies' and 'peelers'. It is occasionally open to the public.

Leave not by the continuing moor-edge track, but a nicer path heading north across the moor past a crater by the tower. This runs to a kissing-gate in a fence, then continues north to approach a reedy saddle in front of Harcles Hill. Just short of the dip take a branch left, rising gently alongside the reedy beginnings to level out on the flat moor top. Approaching steeper flanks overlooking the valley of Red Brook, a path merges from the left and then your path bears right on a gentle curve to rapidly fork. Best choice is the left one, which drops slightly before contouring round the steeper slope. Traversing on by boulders and small quarrying scars, you meet a broader path coming up from a flagpole by a gate below. An MOD warning sign is the first of many that shadow the next stage, though you remain outside the firing range. Turn right up this, with grand views into the dalehead. At the top the path crosses Holcombe Moor to a cross-paths at Pilgrims' Cross, overlooked by a flagpole. The informative stone occupies the site of an ancient cross.

Resume straight on with the signs on a brief final rise to a brow beneath another flagpole. The path runs grandly on, angling gently down to leave MOD territory. At a fork drop right to an outer wall corner, and descend between converging walls to leave the moor at a farm track (Moor Road) by spoil heaps. Turn right along the broad track to quickly reach the old farm at Chatterton Close. Keep straight on to a gate at the end back onto the moor. A cart track runs a lengthy course along its base (mostly with verges) to become briefly enclosed at houses at Higher Tops. Emerging back onto a corner of the moor, you are joined by other tracks to slant left off the moor, becoming enclosed. With the church spire ahead, remain on this to the main road opposite the Shoulder of Mutton pub. Just yards short of the road take a setted road past a fine old house on the right. Just beyond, Cross Lane is joined to run past further characteristic properties, rejoining the outward route just two minutes from the start.

Peel Tower from the start point

4¼ miles from Jumbles Country Park

A wealth of historic interest beyond a popular reservoir's country park

Start *Jumbles Country Park (SD 735139; BL2 4JS), water company car park off A676*
Map *OS Explorer 287, West Pennine Moors*

Jumbles Reservoir dates from 1971, and with refreshments and WC its country park is a popular location in the Bradshaw Valley. From the far (south) end of the car park a path drops (briefly splitting) through trees to a junction, where go straight down to a footbridge on Bradshaw Brook beneath the grassy dam. Across, a broad path bears left through trees, rising slightly into the more open Ouzel Nest Meadows. Reaching a corner, it swings right to briefly rise to a kissing-gate onto Grange Road. Turn right between fields and prestigious dwellings to end at Grange Farm. Continue straight on an enclosed way ahead to a gateway into woodland by the reservoir shore. The path runs on, passing a sailing club to a junction in front of a house. Go right to remain by the shore, though just past a parking area the path is deflected left between an old millpond and houses to re-emerge by the shore. Just a short way further is a tall footbridge across the reservoir.

Don't cross, but turn left past a colourful guidepost on a stepped path rising into trees. Emerging, it rises between fields and past a pond to descend past a World War Two pillbox to a stile/gate onto the B6391. Across, trace the footway left the short way to the drive to Turton Tower. Built as an early 15th century defensive pele tower, the black and white farmhouse is an Elizabethan addition. Acquired by the local authority in 1930 it is open to the public, with grounds, shop and tearoom. Keep straight on an access road past the hall to a castellated railway bridge, a 'folly' built by the owner of Turton Tower: the left tower has steps to a viewing platform. The access road climbs from the bridge to a junction where it bends left: here go right along a level field-bottom track. After a few minutes a cross-paths is reached. Turn right through the small gate, and descend pleasantly to a gate at the bottom by the former Turton & Edgworth Station. Over the level-crossing descend setted Station Road: as it swings right on approaching houses, take a level branch path running left to meet High Street in Turton alongside the Chetham Arms pub.

Go right, and immediately after tall-spired St Anne's church, turn left on the drive to the former school. The path performs a novel stepped detour around the gate to resume the short way to the house. Keep right to a gap at the end accessing a small gate, from where a thin path heads left down into undergrowth. Joining a fence on the right, this partly kerbed old schoolchildren's way descends to a stile onto Wellington Road. Cross to the footway and go very briefly left to an enclosed path slanting down onto Vale Street at Turton Bottoms. Your way is right, but first advance 50 yards to appraise 17th century Pack Saddles Bridge on Bradshaw Brook. Vale Street now runs a part setted course past houses to bridge the stream in front of modern housing. Turn right here on a path clinging tightly to the stream through lush greenery, later broadening before arriving at the head of Jumbles Reservoir. Just ahead is the footbridge which you again ignore, simply continuing on the broad shore path back to the start. *Turton Tower*

4¼ miles from Entwistle

An extended circuit of an upland reservoir, visiting gritstone crags in a hidden side valley

Start Entwistle embankment (SD 721172; BL7 0LU), lower car park on Batridge Road off B6391 Greens Arms Road (reached from A666 Blackburn-Bolton road)
Map OS Explorer 287, West Pennine Moors

Cross the road to a kissing-gate sending a broad, firm path left along the south shore of Entwistle Reservoir. Began in 1831 and enlarged in 1840, its full name is Turton & Entwistle Reservoir. A pleasant and popular stroll runs beneath conifers (of which many have been felled) to a reservoir head footbridge on inflowing Cadshaw Brook. Without crossing, a firm path continues upstream the short way to a second footbridge by a ford: you shall return here after a short detour to Cadshaw Rocks. Continue upstream for a further five minutes along the firm concession path into the wooded recesses of Yarnsdale. As it starts a stonier climb away from the stream, a gap reveals Cadshaw Rocks across it. Marked on the map as Fairy Battery, it is said to have been the location of 17th century non-conformist services: it is now a playground of rock climbers. For a closer look, a stepped path drops the short way to natural stepping-stones on the stream, and a path runs the short way ahead to a kissing-gate in a fence. The path continues through bracken to gain the crag. For further interest, back on the stony path you might advance further up it to within two minutes arrive beneath the imposing, craggy face of Cadshaw Quarry.

Return to the footbridge and ford, and immediately across, ignore the broader options in favour of a stile on the left. Just fifty yards upstream, take a stile on the right by the plantation corner, and a path slants up the rough pasture. As it fades at an outer fence corner, bear right on its slender, level course to meet a broad, grassy track. Double back left on this, gently rising with a view left down to Cadshaw Rocks. Good sections of kerbing feature as your excellent old way rises to a stile/gate onto a broad, stony track at Lowe Hill. Turn right, enjoying long easy strides as it rolls on over high ground. Distant views look ahead to Holcombe Moor and the Peel Tower, while Winter Hill rises back to the right. Part way along are glimpses of Entwistle Reservoir. In time you reach a cattle-grid alongside a heather-reclaimed quarry, and drop to farm buildings at Edge Fold. Continue straight down on a colourful, sunken way, dropping right beneath a house as a thinner footpath through scrub to a junction of access roads.

Turn right on narrow Edge Lane to Entwistle, passing the attractive New Hall at the end with its two-storey gabled porch of 1742. Though hidden away from the outside world, Entwistle boasts a railway station and the popular walkers' rendezvous of the Strawbury Duck. It is served by a minor road from Edgworth across the nearby Wayoh Reservoir. Pass round the side of the pub and follow the unsurfaced Overshores Road back to the dam of Entwistle Reservoir, following the road across it to finish.

At Cadshaw Rocks

4^{1}2 miles from Darwen

**An easy walk to a famous
landmark: glorious heather,
woodland and outstanding views**

Start Sunnyhurst Wood
(SD 679224; BB3 0LA),
*Lychgate car park signed on Earnsdale
Road, off A666 on north edge of Darwen*
Map *OS Explorer 287, West Pennine Moors*

Return briefly along the road back to the Sunnyhurst pub,
opposite which an enclosed way climbs between houses, quickly
rising to heathery verges: Darwen Tower appears above. At a
junction at the top, advance through a gateway onto Darwen
Moor. With the tower beckoning, within 100 yards fork right for a
super, prolonged slant across colourful flanks. Much of Lancashire
is on parade, with Bowland's moors beyond Blackburn. Appearing
below is the drained Sunnyhurst Hey Reservoir, with Earnsdale
Reservoir beyond. Meeting a level path at the top, turn left for five
minutes to the 86ft/26m tower. Built in 1898 for Queen Victoria's
Diamond Jubilee, it was restored in 2021. Spiral steps lead to a
viewing platform, while further steps lead to an upper platform.
Distant features range from Snowdonia to the Lakeland Fells.

Leave by a good path directly south across the open moor,
dropping slightly then swinging right in line with Winter Hill's
masts. It runs grandly on to rise gently to a T-junction. Turn right
for a level walk over the heathery watershed to another junction
in front of a fence junction. Turn right on the broad path, dropping
gently away from the fence to soon rejoin it at an old gateway in
it. Here a broad path doubles back left down to a hairpin bend at
a fence corner overlooking Stepback Clough: continue down to a
scant ruin. At the fence corner behind, double back left down a
short path to a lower stile to meet a broad track below. Leaving the

moor go left on this, over the stream and slanting gently right on a broad course through trees. At the end, the right-hand gate sends a grassy cart track down a large, reedy pasture to Hollinshead Terrace. A bridle-gate admits onto the road at Roddlesworth Information Centre with cafe/WC and the Royal Arms.

Leave by a rough road on the other side of the pub to the hamlet of Ryal Fold. Turn left on the drive into a farmyard: Ryal Farm dates from the 17th century. From the gate at the end a walled track leads into a field. Follow the right-hand boundary dropping gently to a dip, then up the other side through an early gate and gorse bushes with views across Earnsdale Reservoir to Darwen Moor. At the end is a small gate/stile onto a junction of ways, where you enter Dean Lane. Turn right down the initially setted wood-edge way to emerge onto a road at the reservoir embankment. Across the road a good path drops into Sunnyhurst Wood. At an early fork keep right on the main path gently down the valley, closing in on the stream. Further, a branch drops right to a footbridge, but keep straight on to pass a reedy pond and bridge. Further again, the main path bridges the beck to run to a bandstand ahead. A visitor centre with WC/refreshments is minutes further, but at the end of this clearing fork right up a clear, thinner path, ignoring an early branch to the right and climbing steeply above Sunnyhurst Clough. Eventually it eases out to a junction, where go left to the entrance lych-gate just yards from the start.

Darwen Tower

4½ miles from Belmont

A short but invigorating ascent of the West Pennine Moors' major hill

Start Hordern Butts Delf (SD 665158; BL7 8AD), car park on Rivington Road half-mile west of village
Map *OS Explorer 287, West Pennine Moors* **Access** *Open access, dogs on leads March to July from summit to Hordern Stoops*

     From the car park use steps down to a path downstream with a tiny brook, rapidly reaching a fork. Keep left, crossing the stream several times to another fork. The left one over the stream is your return, so for now bear right onto a little brow revealing Ward's Reservoir, the 'Blue Lagoon'. This super path undulates through colourful terrain to the dam at the other end. Shortly after the outflow, bear right on the left-hand of two departing paths, crossing open country to join the road on the village edge. Go right past St Peter's church to the junction at the historic Black Dog pub. Turn right along the A675 Bolton road, crossing briefly to a footway just as far as the end of trees. A stile on the right sends a path rising the short way up Hill Top Clough to a stile into rough pasture. A grassy path rises directly and pleasantly between reeds, fading before reaching a fence-stile onto open moor. Go briefly right to resume uphill on an embanked little path, quickly alighting on a broad way slanting right. Belmont Reservoir is seen beyond the village. Built to serve small collieries, this well-engineered route rises infallibly all the way to the top of Winter Hill.

     Through the gate in the watershed fence advance to the service road ahead, with the massive TV mast to your left. Turn right past various other installations to the Ordnance Survey column on the peaty summit. At 1496ft/456m this is the highest point on the West Pennine Moors, and despite man's distractions it has the most extensive of views. A clear day offers distant views to Snowdonia, the Lake District, the Yorkshire Dales and the Peak District: middle distance hill country includes Bowland and Pendle to the north. Resume to the road-end at the last installation, crossing to a kissing-gate in the adjacent fence. Just yards further the ground falls away steeply, and a grooved, fenceside path slants down to the marshy shelf of Winter Hill Flats. Cross this in company with the fence, dropping a little at the end to a kissing-gate onto the crest of the Belmont-Rivington road at Hordern Stoops.

Turn right, quickly leaving by a stile on the left. Winter Hill's masts reach skyward up to the right, while ahead Belmont's church spire returns, quickly joined by the Blue Lagoon. A path contours away, and with an occasional moist moment enjoys a splendid stride, passing an old quarry at Hoar Stones Delf and on to a gate in a sturdy wall. Continuing on it drops gently to a wall-stile ahead, then head away with a fence on a forming green track to a bridle-gate at the end. For the village take the cart track ahead, otherwise turn right down a fieldside concession path to a small gate onto the road by the reservoir foot. A few yards to the right a surfaced shore path briefly shadows the road, soon leading to a good path across open country between the two to return to the path junction just two minutes from the start.

The Black Dog, Belmont

4¼ miles from Rivington

A stiff pull to a celebrated viewpoint, with much else of interest in this country park

Start Great House Barn Visitor Centre (SD 628138; BL6 7SB), car park on Rivington Lane south of Rivington   *Map* OS Explorer 287, West Pennine Moors

The Rivington estate was purchased in 1900 by William Hesketh Lever, best known for his soap 'empire' at Port Sunlight. Later Lord Leverhulme, he created Lever Park and the Terraced Gardens. Great House Barn is a fine cruck-framed barn, now a cafe with information centre alongside. From the bottom end of the car park, take a firm path left immediately after the Go Ape hut. Across a minor wooded sidestream, it runs firmly and broadly on between open pasture and woodland above Lower Rivington Reservoir. Rivington Pike sits on the skyline up to the left. Remain on this to a major cross-paths in trees just 100 yards short of a replica of Liverpool Castle as it stood at the end of the Civil War.

Leave it by the broad carriageway heading into trees, and remain on this until level with Middle Derbyshires car park on the right. Now just 100 yards short of Rivington Lane, bear left on a path to cross it to a bridleway. With a school to the right it ascends a wood edge, then up through trees onto a broad, unmade road. Turn right to meet a narrow road on a bend. Climbing left, when it turns left for Higher Knoll, keep straight on up the lesser path to a gate. A good track ascends two big sheep pastures to a gate onto a rough road. Across, another rough road rises through a gate, and as it swings right to outflank Rivington Pike's highest point, a worn path breaks off for a direct assault on the upper slopes. Sat on top is Rivington Tower of 1733, with sweeping views beyond the reservoir over the plains: just above you are Winter Hill's masts.

Leave by steps down onto the first rough road to rejoin the earlier one. Go right to the Pigeon Tower, a 1910 dovecote above the Terraced Gardens. Though these instructions take a direct route, you could spend longer exploring this fascinating scene. From the tower descend steps around a summer-house to a triple-arched loggia, then left alongside the Italian Lake. Just beyond, turn down by another summer-house, and further steps to bridge an old road and drop beneath an arch to a path junction. Go briefly left down to another junction, where double back right. This slants down to quickly double back left to another fork. While a terrace path goes straight on, continue the descent facing the Ravine, spiralling down to ignore another terrace path left. Your direct path quickly drops more gently left onto a broad pathway, where drop right past the ruins of South Lodge into open pasture. The track descends back into trees, and another junction. Continue down, quickly bearing right to a track at the rear of Rivington Hall, dating from the 1780s. Go right to emerge at Rivington Hall Barn, and possible refreshments.

Cross the car park to a fork of roads: while the drive goes left, take the dead-straight road ahead. Part way on, a firm path branches right across newly planted Chapel House Wood to a kissing-gate onto a road at Chapel House. Turn left down to a junction at the green, with tearoom: alongside are stocks and a Unitarian Chapel of 1703. Continue down the road, turning left on a short drive past the school: just ahead is the Rivington pub. Beyond a parking area the broad path splits. Bear left, then almost at once branch right on a level path that runs on by Rivington Arboretum to return to the start.

The Pigeon Tower

4¼ miles from Knowley

A delightful stroll to a charming hamlet and fine viewpoints

Start Higher House Lane
(SD 602193; PR6 9BU), roadside parking just
off Heapey Road off B6228 out of Chorley
Map OS Explorer 287, West Pennine Moors
Access Open access, dogs on leads (moor section)

Head away from the junction along Higher House Lane, and around a corner past Moody House Farm to a sharp bend. Go straight ahead on Higher Healey's short drive, the track deflecting right outside the grounds. At the end continue on the hedgerowed track rising to Healey Nab's wooded knoll. Just into the wood is a major fork: take the right branch, dropping slightly and running on to quickly reach another fork. Take the broad path slanting left, ignoring cross-paths to emerge into a felled area. Keep on to an old wall, rising left to a cross-paths on the brow of Healey Nab. A path runs a few yards right to the heathery top, where a cairn at 672ft/205m commands views to Rivington Pike and Chorley.

Back at the cross-paths resume with the wall on your right down to the wood corner, and straight ahead to a cross-paths amid bracken. Take the broader path right, winding round past small old quarries to drop to a level bridleway. Go right a few yards to a stile on the left, and slant left down the pasture to a corner stile. A stepped path spirals down a wooded bank to rejoin Higher House Lane at Anglezarke Reservoir. Turn right on the footway over the reservoir head to follow the road away past Waterman's Cottage. Remain on the road climbing steeply past colourful woodland. Easing at Siddow Fold to the right, a kissing-gate on the left sends a thin path rising gradually away with a fence across grassy moor.

At a fence corner another path is joined and followed left along the moor edge with the fence. Though it precludes dramatic views over the edge of heathery Stronstrey Bank, it is nevertheless a grand stride. Towards the end the path bears gently right to pass through a wall-gap, and on through scattered rocks to gently drop to rejoin the fence overlooking an old quarry's sheer walls. The thinner path deviates briefly from the fence to rejoin it at a stile after a second quarry site. Cross and descend steeply with a fence outside the quarry rim. The fence ends on a knoll, but the path continues down to the quarry bowl, then doubles back down through bracken to a stile onto a broad track in the bracken-clad valley. Turn right over a footbridge in open country and along to a larger bridge and path crossroads. Now go left through a kissing-gate, crossing The Goit to emerge at White Coppice's cricket pitch.

Turn left alongside the pitch and away on the rough access road, passing dams on either side and becoming surfaced to enter White Coppice hamlet: a ford and green precede the central junction. Hard to believe this was a hive of 19th century industrial activity. Across the bridge a footbridge sends a path downstream, crossing a footbridge on a sidestream to reach a reservoir head. A super path traces its tree-fringed shore, with a stile at the end onto an embankment between reservoirs. Resume on a broad grassy path along the southern shore of this larger one, and at the end advance straight on to a car park. After the first parking area a path drops right to the corner of a lower dam, slanting down onto Higher House Lane to finish. *Waterman's Cottage, Anglezarke*

4^{1}2 miles from Anglezarke

A splendid reservoir circuit with fine woodland and wide-ranging views

Start Anglezarke Reservoir (SD 619161 PR6 9DQ), water company's large but unsigned Anglezarke Trail car park off Moor Road on eastern shore of reservoir
Map OS Explorer 287, West Pennine Moors

With your back to the car park a surfaced path heads right into trees, forking left to drop gently to a lower path. Double back left onto a broad, tarmac way, going right with the reservoir wall. This heads round past an inlet to climb briefly to a hairpin bend: here branch left on a good path contouring around above the water. Through a bridle-gate it runs nearer the wood top through springtime bluebells, ultimately dropping to a cross-paths with a broader way. Go left along to a kissing-gate into open pasture, a lovely section with big reservoir views. At the far end is a kissing-gate into a wood top, leading along to one onto a road. Go left past isolated Waterman's Cottage, a roadside footway crossing the reservoir head to a kissing-gate on the left to begin the return.

A path runs above the shoreline wall through Grey Heights Wood before rising in gentle, sometimes muddy, stages to a bridle-gate into a field. 50 yards across it is a kissing-gate onto Heapey Fold Lane. Go left on this unmade road with big, open views. When it turns sharp right, keep on the bridleway ahead to join a drive at Kays Farm. Go right to a road, then left past several dwellings beneath Charnock Embankment. When the road enters trees, take a stile/gate on the left and cross to a stile from where a path runs with a wall, soon swinging left to approach the shore. This splendid final section is later deflected by woodland to a kissing-gate onto a road: the Yew Tree Inn is two minutes to the right at Lane Ends. Go left on the embankment and remain on the footway around to the junction at the car park access road.